Presented to

_____

on this, your confirmation day,

_____

I thank my God every time I remember you.
In all my prayers for all of you, I always pray
with joy because of your partnership in the
gospel from the first day until now, being con-
fident of this, that He who began a good work
in you will carry it on to completion until the
day of Christ Jesus. *Philippians 1:3–6*

Confirmed in Christ

Roy G. Gesch

CONCORDIA PUBLISHING HOUSE · SAINT LOUIS

Copyright © 1983, 1997 Concordia Publishing House.
3558 S. Jefferson Avenue, St. Louis, MO 63118-3968
Manufactured in the United States of America

Library of Congress Cataloging-in-Publication Data

Gesch, Roy G.
    Confirmed in Christ/Roy G. Gesch. — Rev. ed.
        p.   cm.
    Summary: A spiritual guide for young people intended
to help them examine their religious training and how it
can be applied to their adult life.
    ISBN 0-570-04962-8
    1. Youth—Religious life. [1. Conduct of life. 2. Christian
life.] I. Title.
BV4850.G395   1997
248.8'3—dc20
                                                      96-38785

---

8 9 10   06 05 04

Many thanks to the students, teachers, and principals of Orange County Lutheran High School in Orange, California, and California Lutheran High School in Tustin, California, who generously shared their time, thoughts, and feelings with the author.

Contents

Confirmation—What Does It Really Mean?

You're confirmed. Congratulations! Your confirmation day was probably one of the happiest days of your life—a day filled with inspiring and memorable events. But what does this special day really mean?

For your parents, your family, and your friends, your confirmation was the fulfillment of their hopes and dreams. Through the years, they've invested a lot of love and prayer in you. With God's help, your parents have faithfully followed His instructions to "train a child in the way he should go" (Proverbs 22:6). As you stood in front of the whole church and confessed what you believe about God and as you promised to love and remain loyal to Him, they must have felt that God had answered their prayers. He had blessed their love and effort. He had brought you into a closer relationship with Himself.

At your confirmation, the whole church shared in your joy and confession. For your fellow church members, it was another sign that God is at work in your life. Some of these people have watched you grow in your life as a fellow believer from your Baptism until now! It must mean so much to them to hear you confess the faith they share with you. Think how they must rejoice as they kneel with you at the Lord's altar to be strengthened and reassured by the body and blood of Christ.

Is your confirmation a joyful time for you? It definitely should be. You're probably relieved that there won't be any more conflicts with after-school or weekend activities, not to mention that you won't have any more memory work assignments.

But what does your confirmation really mean to you? This special day—when you confess your faith before God, your family, and your fellow believers—should bring you great happiness. During your preparation for this day, you have come to know God better. You have become more aware of what God has been doing and continues to do for you. You have come to realize His great love in Jesus Christ and His power in your life. You have developed an earnest desire to live to the fullest the new life He has given you in your Baptism.

Your greatest joy about your confirmation centers in the fact that you told God how much He means to you. You confessed the faith He put in your heart. At your Baptism, your sponsors and family confessed their faith in front of everyone. Now you have confirmed this faith in God before Him and His people without embarrassment or fear. You have showed that now, as a teenager, and later, as an adult, you are looking to God's Holy Spirit to help you follow His path.

Yes, your confirmation day may be over, but what happened—your confession and the faith that caused it—hasn't ended. Your confirmation was only another step in growing up in Christ. It's a little like an egg. An egg can't fly. Yet the living thing in that egg has wings. If that life is cared for, one day it will fly.

Until now people have seen you as a child. And they've probably treated you as one. But now your day has come. You have broken out of your childhood shell. Your confirmation classes were like flying lessons. You were being shown how to use the wings of faith that God gave you.

At your Baptism, your parents made a promise. They kept that promise as they taught you about Jesus and took you to church and Sunday school. With God's help, they did their part to get you into the air. God worked through your parents, your teachers, and your pastor to prepare you for your solo flight, your public confession of faith in Him.

Now you can fly. But you don't fly alone. Jesus flies with you. He is the one that gives you the spiritual maturity and the faith to tell the whole world that you are His child. Your confirmation marks the day that you took control of your relationship with Jesus. You are saying to your family, "Thanks for your love and your training, but I'm going to stand on my own two feet. With Jesus' help, I'm going to wing it by myself." As you confirmed the promise they once made for you, you took on yourself the responsibility for keeping that promise. And Jesus promises to be with you always and provide His Holy Spirit to guide your flight.

But getting in the air isn't the big thing. It's strong flying that's important. Ask Jesus to help you use your wings in the right way and to fly in the directions He wants you to take.

Confirmation is also like baseball. Until now you've been learning the game. Confirmation class has been spring training. Now you're in the Big Leagues. You may be a rookie, but rookies win games. Every player has the potential to be the most valuable player.

But watch out! Don't let the pressures of the big leagues knock you out of the game. You don't want to be one of the many one-hit wonders or one-season marvels that fill the record books. Ask God to give you a strong faith, one that will stick with it and enjoy a long career. Ask Him to bring you safely to His heavenly Hall of Fame.

2

You're Someone Special!

The original painting of "Washington Crossing the Delaware" hangs in a New York City gallery. It's so big that it covers an entire wall. As soon as you walk into the room, you begin studying the details, including Washington's nose and the oars of the boat. But the details aren't really that exciting. What's really impressive is what you see when you step out of the room. Then the full dramatic effect of the size and detail takes over.

The same thing happens as you observe Salvador Dali's picture of Lincoln. You absolutely cannot make out Lincoln's features if you stand too close. But from 20 feet or more away, Lincoln's face jumps out right at you.

When you get so focused on the details, you can miss the big picture. It happens in real life, just like it does in those examples from the art world. For a time, teaching and learning all the *pieces* of information can obscure the overall impact the subject has on your life.

Think about science class, especially when you learned about the human body. It's hard to keep a complete picture in your mind of the wonderful body God gave you as you zero in on the details of arteries and veins, muscles and tissues, organs and glands. Or think about a choir or band practice when you worked on individual parts. By itself, each instrument or vocal part sounded weak, but when combined, the full choir or band made beautiful music.

If one thing should have come through loud and clear in the details *and* in the "big picture" of confirmation class, it's that you're special. Maybe you didn't feel special when you couldn't quite memorize the meaning to the First Article. Or maybe all those tests just seemed to prove that everyone wanted to make your life difficult. But you *are* someone special to your parents, your church, and most important, to God.

I can imagine one "detail" that may have made you feel anything but special: learning the Ten Commandments. Studying God's Law can make you feel like you did when your mom told you Grandma was on her way over just as you walked in from cutting the lawn. You ran upstairs and looked in the mirror. Your face was sweaty, your hair had grass in it, and your clothes and legs were filthy. You didn't feel like anyone—even your grandma—could love you or think you were special. And that's how the Ten Commandments can make you feel—dirty and unworthy of any special treatment from God.

Or what about studying the Apostles' Creed? It's hard to imagine that God has time for *you*. After all, He has billions of other people to look out for. Some are richer, better looking, smarter, more athletic, or even more needy than you. As you look at the "details" of God's work on your behalf, it can be hard to grasp that He's doing all this for *you* because you are someone very special to Him.

As you learned more about God—who He is, what He's like, and what He has done and is doing—you explored some wonderful but very deep truths. It can be difficult to wrap your mind around all the pieces of information and still keep in mind that God cares about you. In fact, all the information you're learning about God is like learning to scuba dive. Even if you try to explore deep in the ocean, you'll never learn everything about the sea. The vastness of God's power and attributes—like the vastness of the ocean—makes you feel like an insignificant cork bobbing around in the Pacific.

It's amazing that the more you learn about God, the greater He becomes and the smaller you feel. You may start to think that you can't be special to Him because you're just a kid. You're not even an adult, let alone an angel or some other "perfect" creature. But you're missing the big picture. Remember what it says in Martin Luther's explanation of the Third Article?

> I believe that I cannot by my own reason or strength believe in Jesus Christ, my Lord, or come to Him; but the Holy Spirit has called me by the Gospel, enlightened me with His gifts, sanctified and kept me in the true faith.

God thinks you are special enough. He's already shown you how special you are to Him. He sent Jesus to be your Savior. He sent His Holy Spirit to work faith in your heart. He's kept you in that faith so you could confess it in front of your church. Repeat after me: I, _____ , am very special to God!

Let's run through some of the things you have learned that will explain the big picture of God's love for you. In the process, you'll also see your special role in that big picture.

You learned that there is only one God. No doubt you had probably already picked that up on your own. After all, isn't that the only thing that really makes any sense? Well, way back when the Egyptians were building the pyramids, God wanted all people to know this truth. He commanded Moses to proclaim: "Hear, O Israel: The LORD our God, the LORD is one" (Deuteronomy 6:4). Centuries later, when the Greeks and Romans were busy worshiping a whole group of good-for-nothing gods, God's Holy Spirit inspired Paul and the other apostles to make it clear to the world again that "there is no God but one" (1 Corinthians 8:4).

Because God considers you to be very special, He made sure that you know this "detail"—and that you know Him. It's sad that so many people grope around in the dark, looking for God in crystals and drugs and new religions. They say they want to know the *truth,* but they refuse to believe the truth God tells them in the Bible. These people think they know better than God. They fall for the same superstitious garbage that captured minds in the Dark Ages. Some even make up their own religion. "It has to suit me," they say. Some look to the stars to govern their life or turn to some telephone psychic. If someone asks you what sign you were born under, answer them honestly, "The sign of the cross." Tell them about the one true God who has sent His Son to save the world and who loves you personally.

There's another way that God shows how special you are to Him. When God shows Himself to you as He really is, He doesn't want you to think of Him as some great, untouchable Person or Force. He doesn't want His greatness to make you cringe or grovel. What He wants is your love. He invites you to love Him "with all your heart and with all your soul and with all your strength" (Deuteronomy 6:5; Matthew 22:37). Luther said it so clearly when he described our relationship with God as "dear children" who have a "dear Father." Now that is truly something special!

But that's only scratching the surface. You also learned from the Bible what God has been doing for you. Those acts and actions shout how highly God regards you—how special you are to Him. Take a good look at yourself. The fact that you were born, that God gave you life and new life in Baptism, that you are a member of your family and His family, proves that God loves you and has a special plan for you.

Take a good look at your body. Your brain is far more complex than the best computer. It even can out-think a computer when you develop it to its full potential. (If you don't believe me, check out the 1996 chess duel between "Deep Blue," a chess-playing computer, and grand master chess champion Gary Kasparov.) The best cameras run a poor second to your eyes, even if you need corrective lenses. Stereo sound systems attempt to match your ears' ability to hear. The most high-tech coverings can't come close to your skin and its toughness, tenderness, or its remarkable ability to heal. And they can't feel or perspire. None of the other living things that God put on this world can think or dream or invent. God made human beings different; He made us special.

And in this entire world of special human beings, you are one of a kind. To God, you are not just part of the crowd. He knows you personally. He told the prophet Jeremiah, "Before I formed you in the womb I knew you, before you were born I set you apart" (Jeremiah 1:5). And it's the same for you. What could be more special than that?

But as wonderful as your unique body and the gift of life are, it wouldn't mean much if you had to enjoy them by yourself. God has enriched your life with family and friends, food and home, a beautiful world, and opportunities to learn and grow and to work and play. And that's only the beginning of what God has done for you.

The most important thing that reveals how special you are in God's sight is something you've just confessed to believe. God sent His Son, Jesus, to die and rise again for *you*. Even though you were and are a sinner, Jesus took your punishment for your sins and gave you new life. God sent His Holy Spirit to work faith in your heart at your Baptism. And God has continued to strengthen that faith through your parents, friends, teachers, and pastors. He has brought you to this moment, when you confessed your faith. And God will continue to walk with you throughout your life because you are special to Him.

3

Jesus—Your Special Friend

"Tell me who your friends are, and I'll tell you who you are." That's a true statement. You can tell a lot about people and their lives by the kind of friends they have. Although you don't need a lot of friends, you do need at least one friend you can trust, someone who won't let you down when you need him or her the most.

Friendship is an important part of the Good News you've learned in confirmation class. You learned that you have a very special friend—Jesus. The statement of faith and the promise you made at your confirmation indicates that you know Jesus is your friend. In fact, you know He's the most important friend you have.

But you need to remember that Jesus' willingness to be your friend shows that *you* are very special to Him. And Jesus isn't just willing to be your friend, He has chosen you. He *wants* to be your friend. And being the kind of friend you need, one you can always depend on, cost Jesus a lot. It cost Him His life.

Much More Than a Pen Pal

Many years ago, two elementary school English teachers started a pen pal program between students in their classes. The students—including two girls—drew names and began writing. One girl lived on a farm in Iowa; the other lived in a small town in Maine. While most of their classmates wrote a few letters and quit, these two girls continued to write to each other.

A strong friendship developed between the pen pals. They exchanged pictures and shared secrets. They discussed their lives at school and at home. The two girls shared their pastimes, their feelings, and their major life events. As they grew older, they opened their hearts and helped each other with the disappointments and aches that no one else knew. Soon the two were writing about dates and going steady and eventually about weddings and babies.

Finally, after 15 years of correspondence, the husbands of the two women suggested they actually meet. The woman from Iowa made the trip to the home of her longtime pen pal in Maine. A television news program recorded the meeting. The two women recognized each other immediately at the airport and rushed into each other's arms.

What a visit these friends had! They never stopped talking. They relived all the events and feelings they had written about over the years. The days flew by. Soon it was time to say good-bye. As they parted at the airport, both women agreed that they had considered the other a close friend for years. They also admitted that feeling was nothing compared to the joy of actually being together. Seeing each other in the flesh was much more powerful than sharing words on paper. It was an opportunity to really share each other's lives.

That's what's so remarkable about Jesus. Throughout the Bible, God tells you that He loves you and that you are special to Him. He describes the big plans He has for you. He emphasizes that He won't let anything interfere with those plans. And throughout the Bible, God proves again and again that He has the power and love to make those plans happen. Just think about Noah, Abraham and Sarah, Moses, David, Elizabeth and Zechariah, and Mary.

Unfortunately, many people in the Bible thought that God's communication with them was like being a pen pal. After reading a few "letters" from God, they got tired or bored. They didn't bother to keep in touch with God. So God fulfilled His greatest plan. He realized words were not enough so He sent *the* Word to earth—Jesus Christ.

Even before He made the world, God planned this meeting. Being fully aware that none of us could keep in touch with Him on our own, God planned to come to us. God came to us through Jesus. And it was more than a chance meeting. Jesus came to be one of us at the right time—the time God chose. Because Jesus chose to leave heaven and spend His life with us, because He came to earth specifically to *give* His life for us, we get a small sense of and appreciation for the depth of His friendship.

Think of Christmas. Your joy centers around the beautiful story of Jesus' birth. You anticipate the celebration. Perhaps you felt the excitement as you donned a costume and took your place as an angel, shepherd, or Wise Man at the side of the manger in the Christmas service. Though you gradually gave up those roles to younger children, you didn't lose the joy of hearing and singing about how Jesus came to be your Savior. Nor is Christmas any less wonderful now. In fact, the older you get, the more awesome it becomes and the more you appreciate the way God planned everything.

Jesus didn't come in a spaceship to set up an office in the penthouse of some magnificent skyscraper so He could control all nations and all people. He could have, you know. Everything is rightly His. But the chances are pretty slim that you would be able to think of Jesus as a personal friend if He were so far removed from your everyday existence.

The genius of God's plan was that humble, lowly birth. That Baby was God in the flesh—weak, poor, dependent, suffering all the chills and discomforts you could ever experience. Jesus came to endure the worst so you could enjoy the best. He came to be with His human creatures. He came to be one of us. More than that, Jesus came to serve us. He felt our hurts. He faced our temptations. He took the burden and penalty of our sins. Jesus did for us what we could not do for ourselves. Jesus came to sacrifice His life in our place. He took the penalty for our sin so we, His forgiven friends, might live with Him forever. What an amazing Friend!

A Picture of Friendship

Remember the proverb "A picture is worth a thousand words"? Jesus is that picture! He is *the* living proof that God really loves you, that you are special to God. When the world gets so hectic and so noisy, you have trouble hearing what God is saying. Your sinful self turns you into a pretty poor listener. But *seeing* is another matter.

The disciples saw Jesus during His life, when He died, and after His resurrection. You have their eyewitness accounts to prove that Jesus is your best friend. And God sends His Holy Spirit to open the eyes of your heart to see Jesus as your personal Savior, as your personal friend.

As you read your Bible, you *see* with the eyes of faith as Jesus touches the eyes of a blind man and heals him. That's love and power in action. You *see* with the eyes of faith as Jesus touches and opens the ears of a deaf man. That's love and power in action. You *see* with the eyes of faith as Jesus straightens and gives strength to crippled legs. That's love and power that go far beyond anything you can offer to others. "God is love." In Jesus, you *see* God's love in action.

Hopefully, you didn't see those things and say, "Hooray for them! Once upon a time all sorts of good things happened because Jesus was around when people needed Him." Jesus' love and power are for you too—for all of us—for all time. That's the message of the cross: Christ "loved [you] and gave Himself for [you]" (Galatians 2:20). That's the message of the empty grave: Jesus lives, and you too will live! Or in Jesus' own words, "Because I live, you also will live" (John 14:19).

A Friend Who Does Everything

One preacher put it this way, "What Jesus has done for others, He can do for you!" But it's even better than that. What He's done for others, Jesus *has* done and *is still doing* for you. Why? Because Jesus is your special friend.

Sure, sometimes you'll get confused. You won't always see your goals clearly. You might get mixed signals. You won't always be sure where you are or where you should go. You'll cry out, "God, please show me the way." That's when your best Friend comes to you and says, "I am the way."

Sometimes you'll get totally upset about things you read or hear. People—sometimes even your friends or teachers—will contradict what the Bible says. People you respect and believe to be experts will argue with each other, each claiming the other is wrong. You'll cry out, "God, what is the truth?" That's when your best Friend comes to you and says, "I am the truth."

Sometimes you'll be frightened by what's going on around you. Will there be another war? Can you make the right decisions for your life? Will you live long enough to see your grandchildren? You'll cry out, "God, I want to live!" That's when your best Friend comes to you and says, "I am the life."

One of the first Bible verses you ever learned was probably John 3:16. In that one passage, God ties together and summarizes the wonderful Good News about Jesus. Say it. Do more than that—personalize it.

> For God so loved *me*, _____ , that He gave His one and only Son, that *I*, _____ , believing in Him, shall not perish but have eternal life.

When you believe that, when you trust in that statement, you know the most important fact of life: God loves *you*. He sent Jesus to be your special friend. Jesus is the greatest proof that you are truly special to God.

But there's one more thing that makes this friendship with Jesus wonderful. Earthly friends sometimes have a bad habit of disappearing just when you need them most. But not Jesus! Your special Friend made this promise to you: "Surely I am with you always to the very end of the age" (Matthew 28:20). And Jesus *never* goes back on His word.

4

You've Got a Lot to Live For!

You've probably heard the phrase a thousand times, "You've got a lot to live for!" Advertisers seem to use it often as they try to sell things to teenagers. Commercials illustrating the phrase usually show happy groups of gorgeous young people surfing, sailing, playing sports, or taking part in some activity that shows people enjoying life. The not-so-hidden message is that life is meant to be lived to the fullest.

Before you ignore that message, let's look at it from another angle. "You've got a lot to live for" is the key message for young Christians too. As you celebrate your confirmation, your entry into the "adult" church, don't look back. Don't think of confirmation as completing something. Look ahead. This is just the beginning. You've got a lot to live for!

The teenage years are a wonderful time of life. You'll learn and grow, explore new paths, try new ideas, find (and probably lose) new loves. You'll experience sports and dates and parties. You'll accept responsibility for personal decisions. You'll set and accept personal challenges. In general, you'll explore and enjoy the world around you as you never have before.

But just in case you're getting a little self-assured, remember, no one said it would be easy. You'll run into people—adults—who have become cynical with age. They would agree with the playwright George Bernard Shaw that "youth is wasted on young people." They covet (remember that word from confirmation class?) your strength and vitality. Some adults can make it pretty rough for young people. They read about juvenile delinquency and gangs and because some teenagers are irresponsible, they form a negative opinion about all youth—even you.

For example, a woman in her 60s parked her car on the street in front of her home. She opened her door to get out without checking for approaching traffic. Unfortunately, she opened her door right in front of a car driven by a boy coming home from high school. It was her fault. She admitted it was her fault. But as people passed the accident scene, several drivers could be heard muttering something about "teenage drivers."

You can probably tell your own stories about friends who have been put down just because they're young. Maybe it's even happened to you. But don't go through your teenage years with a chip on your shoulder. Remember what the apostle Paul wrote to his younger friend Timothy:

> Don't let anyone look down on you because you are young, but set an example for the believers in speech, in life, in love, in faith and in purity. *1 Timothy 4:12*

Paul wrote to Timothy the same thing that your parents, pastors, and friends are saying to you. Don't drop out because the going gets rough. Don't quit because people won't give you the chance you want and deserve. You're someone special. You are in what could be—and should be—the best years of your life. You've got a lot to live for! Live it up!

Having a good life certainly means more than *collecting* things. Clothes, cars, in-line skates, computers, jewelry, video games, and stereos may be considered part of the good life, but there's certainly a lot more to it than that.

Having a good life also means more than *doing* things. Dates, parties, proms, athletic contests, vacations, and shopping might be favorite activities and important parts of your life, but you know there's more to living than that.

Neither collecting things nor doing things has much to do with being a special person. You might be above average if you have lots of things or participate in tons of activities. And it's great to get straight *As,* achieve all-conference in a sport, be voted most popular, or enjoy a well-paying weekend job. These things count for something. They add zest to life. But none of them brings or guarantees lasting happiness.

If you really think about it, people who depend on collecting or doing to have a good life end up with little more than a few pictures and clippings, some trophies gathering dust on a shelf, a couple certificates of achievement, or some flowers pressed in an old book. Their life becomes focused on memories. Occasionally it's fun to look back, but memories can be depressing. They can become reminders of how much things have changed. You might discover you've become one more name in a long list of homecoming queens, trophy winners, promising students, or star athletes.

However, as God's special person living the life that God has given you, you get an extra dimension to life. There's a lot more to being a Christian and living as God's special child than the world will ever know. *You* need to know and appreciate what it means to be special to God and to have a special life to live.

Your New Life

God made you different. He gave you something extra. No, not three eyes or 12 fingers! Physically you aren't any different from other human beings. But inside, in your heart, you are completely different. God gave you a whole new life—a life of faith. It's more than just the assurance that because of Jesus you will live forever with God in heaven after your earthly life is over. God gave you a new life that you, as a Christian, live right now!

Jesus said your new life begins with a second birth—being "born of water and the Spirit" (John 3:5). Paul puts it this way: "If anyone is in Christ, he is a new creation" (2 Corinthians 5:17). Through the waters of Baptism, you completely passed from something old to something new. You passed from being "dead to God" to being God's chosen child. What an awesome thought!

This second birth is like a butterfly emerging from a cocoon. From the moment the egg was laid, the creature was meant to be a butterfly. But initially, crawling around as a caterpillar, there were few clues to its eventual form. Its life as a butterfly is completely new and different from its life as a caterpillar.

Unlike the caterpillar, your new life in Christ wasn't inside you before. God's Holy Spirit came into your life in Baptism and caused you to be born or created all over again. In the water and the Word, God made you the special person He planned for you to be at the beginning of the world. Only God could do this.

Unlike the caterpillar, you couldn't make that change to a new life by yourself. You couldn't even *want* to change. Again, remember what you confessed: "I believe that I cannot by my own reason or strength believe in Jesus Christ, my Lord, or come to Him." The Holy Spirit brought you to faith through God's Word in Baptism. And He will continue to nurture and strengthen your faith through the years.

Through Baptism, God made you spiritually alive. In this new life, by God's grace, you are dead to sin but totally alive to God. As you learned about God from parents, teachers, and pastors, the Holy Spirit kept your faith alive. As you learned in confirmation class, God works through the Word and Sacraments to reaffirm and build up your faith. Every time you read your Bible or come to His table, God works to keep you connected to Him as His special child. He helps you enjoy the new life He's given you.

This new life isn't an add-on. It's a whole new you. You can't cut your life apart, separating your spiritual life from your physical life. You can't say that church and Sunday school, confirmation class, church youth group, family devotions, and your personal Bible study and prayer time make up your new life with God and the rest of the time—at school, home, work, or play—you get to live your old life. Being alive in Christ involves the *whole* you.

Alive God's Way

You've probably already discovered that being alive in Christ is an all-out, exciting way to live. It affects you totally. Christ affects what you do and how you do it. He influences your every thought and attitude. Unfortunately, some people—even your friends—just don't understand. They think that living a Christ-centered life will cramp your style, cut into your ability to have fun, hold you back, make you a real drag. They don't want you to miss out on all the fun.

But it's not true! Living as God wants you to live may mean some changes and different ways to make choices, but will you really miss out? *No way!* Giving up things that don't do you any good can hardly be considered missing out. Just think about what it means to be alive God's way. If you are looking for one simple phrase to sum it up, use Paul's "Rejoice in the Lord always" (Philippians 4:4). Living God's way means knowing you are right with God through Jesus Christ. You don't need to be worried about a guilty conscience. You don't need to be afraid to look God, your parents, or anyone else in the eye. You know, no matter what, you are God's forgiven child.

Being alive God's way gives you the power to break bad habits. You just have to ask God for His help. And when you ask, God can even help you avoid starting bad habits in the first place.

When you live God's way, you don't get bogged down with fears and anxieties. You know God cares for you. You don't have to be afraid of today, tomorrow, or even of death. You know that Jesus, who has already conquered everything for you—even death—will be with you all the way.

That's a quick look at the new life God gave you when the Holy Spirit brought you to faith in Jesus through the Word and Baptism. This new life is yours to live *now* in all its fullness, and it's not going to change as you get older. No one can take this life away from you. It's yours—now and always.

That makes you a truly special person. Your new life makes you different from most of the people in the crowds around you. Alive in Christ, you are priceless. God has given you tremendous worth. As a little child, you may have chosen shiny copper pennies over dirty silver dollars, but don't make that mistake with your new life in Christ. Because God made you special, you've got a lot to live for! Thank God for that. Live your new life and enjoy it!

5

God Isn't Finished with You Yet

In the world of music, several beautiful compositions are called "unfinished" symphonies. While music lovers enjoy them, you can't help wondering how much more beautiful they might have been if they had been finished. Just like the "unfinished" music pieces, artists collect "unfinished" sketches. Sometimes the sketches are just exercises to practice drawing shapes or to learn how to make shading look natural. Sometimes the sketches are rough ideas for future paintings. Art lovers treasure Leonardo da Vinci's sketches. They're even willing to pay a big price to own one. When you look at da Vinci's finished work, like the

Last Supper, you can't help wishing that some of his sketches might have been developed further.

If you wander around Italy, you come across a number of Michelangelo's fantastic statues. Some, like *David,* are so famous that you see copies of them around the world. Pictures of them appear in almost every art book. But even more interesting than the finished statues are the huge blocks of marble with just a part of the human body emerging from the stone. One such block shows only a completed muscular arm and shoulder. Another features a leg. These chunks of marble reveal only a glimpse of the body that's locked in the stone. Each statue is perfect, as far as it's developed. You can use your imagination to try and complete it, but you end up wishing the sculptor had finished the project. Who knows what might have happened—the statue could have become even more magnificent than *David.*

Just like these unfinished symphonies and sketches and statues, your life is filled with unlimited possibilities. Your whole life is an exciting adventure—not just some day but right now. Americans say, "Isn't it wonderful to be born in this land of opportunity? Just think, anyone can grow up to become president!" While this may be a truthful statement, there's only one president elected every four years. That doesn't open the door to very many people in a land of more than 200 million.

When you talk about the potential that God has given you, however, you're not fighting against bad odds. God has given you a wonderful new life, and He promises to help you live it to the fullest. That means you're assured of making it—of winning—right from the start.

Headed in the Right Direction

Dear friends, now we are children of God, and what we will be has not yet been made known. But we know that when He appears, we shall be like Him, for we shall see Him as He is. *1 John 3:2*

You've no doubt seen or heard the saying, "Be patient! God isn't finished with me yet." What it really says is "Look, I'm not perfect. Please don't expect me to be perfect. But I'm on my way. God's taking me in the right direction. He and I are working on it every day. By God's grace, and with your love and encouragement, I will become the person God and you and I want me to be."

No, you may not be perfect. You haven't achieved your full potential, but neither has anyone else. Don't forget that! Look around. There are some people—not many, but a few—that you consider pretty close to perfect. Maybe the list includes your grandfather, an understanding pastor, a super-fair teacher, or a Christian friend who really lives by the Book. But not one of those people has truly arrived at perfection. They're still on the way too. God isn't done with them either.

One day, you—and they—will arrive. But for now "what we will be has not yet been made known." Think about that. Let your imagination run wild. Don't just think about what you'll be like when you're with Jesus. Think about what you can become, by God's grace, right now, right here on earth. That's really exciting!

Becoming Involves Growth

If your family is like most, you have a door frame. You know the one—it has marks all up and down where your parents measured your height. You always felt you were growing so slowly. Everything seemed the same day after day. Then suddenly Mom or Dad would exclaim with great surprise, "My, how you've grown!" Then they'd get you next to the door frame and put the next little mark above the last. And sure enough, you'd grown an inch or two or maybe even three. No one should have been surprised that you'd grown. It had been happening all along. But the mark on the door frame confirmed it. It showed that you had made real progress.

That's what's happening in your new life in Christ too—at least it should be. You should be growing stronger and becoming more mature in your faith than you were a year ago. And you should become still stronger and more mature in Christ next year. Ask God to help you follow His way and to send His Spirit to strengthen you and move you toward a more mature faith.

You may not always feel like you've grown in your faith. Don't let that discourage you. Spiritual growth isn't as easy to measure as physical growth. You can't mark it on a wall because it's happening inside you. God is making changes in your mind and will. Your attitudes, words, and deeds give clues to what is happening on the inside, but even they don't tell the whole story.

At certain times in your life, you can expect rapid growth. Physically, you are in the middle of one of those cycles right now. You've probably shot up in height. Your body and muscles are filling out—hopefully in the right directions! Everyone around you can see that you are no longer a child. A growth in your appetite goes hand in hand with that growth spurt. Your parents are probably complaining about being eaten out of house and home and threatening to put a lock on the refrigerator. They don't really mean it. Your parents realize your body needs more food because it's burning it faster as your body and mind work harder. When you get hungry, your body is telling you that it's time for another fill-up. It's a sign that you are normal and healthy.

Your new life in Christ will include growth spurts and an increased appetite too. Right now you probably are experiencing rapid growth in your faith. Especially in these last several years, you have become much more aware of the world around you. You have probably also done a lot of thinking about God. You've come up with a lot of questions and now you need some answers.

Think about it this way. An electrical engineer was sitting in his living room reading the newspaper. "Dad, how does the TV work," his 3-year-old son asked. The father was delighted. Finally his son was old enough to take an interest in the wonders of electronics. So the father started explaining signals and waves, circuits and tuners, and picture tubes.

That's when the man's wife, who had been listening to the conversation, came storming into the room. She glared at her husband, walked over to the TV, pushed the "On" button, and told the boy, "There! That's how it works."

"Thanks, Mom!" the boy replied and settled down to watch his program—leaving Dad very confused.

As a child, you weren't too concerned about getting answers. At least not very involved answers. Consider what St. Paul wrote about our attitude as children:

> When I was a child, I talked like a child, I thought like a child, I reasoned like a child. When I became a man, I put childish ways behind me. *1 Corinthians 13:11*

That's what's happening to you right now. You're no longer willing to believe everything everybody tells you. You want some real answers, and you want to be sure those answers are right. You want to explore. Your mind wants to reach where it has never reached before. And that's good! That's your growing intellectual appetite. But you're spiritually hungry too. Everything in you tells you that you need good, nutritious food.

Unfortunately, many people know you are hungry. They have a ready supply of spiritual junk food to share with you. Most cults and new religions aim their messages directly at young people. They offer easy answers to life's complex problems.

They promise a stronger love and more security than what you have at home or in your present church. They offer inside information on how to get along with God.

But junk food is junk food, no matter how attractively it's packaged. The new life God has given you will never meet its full potential on a junk-food diet. Only God, who made you and gave you new life in Christ, can answer your questions. He will give you the healthy food and spiritual vitamins you need to keep your faith strong. He clearly tells you: "I have set before you life and death, blessings and curses. Now choose life" (Deuteronomy 30:19).

Your parents and your church understand the importance of good spiritual food. That's why they've made the effort to teach you God's Word. That's why the church has provided confirmation classes and Sunday school and other group activities. You are growing spiritually, and you need more food than ever before. You are asking more questions, and your church wants you to know where to find the answers. Maybe it seems that you got more answers than you were looking for when you sat in confirmation class. Maybe you weren't ready to handle all the answers. But thank God that He has given you people to point you in the right direction when you do need those answers.

As you continue to grow in your faith, you will think about and ask even more questions. Many prayers will be answered if you have learned to ask God for guidance and help instead of people who know less than you do or have no relationship with God. In the Scriptures and the Sacraments, God provides rich food for your new life. In His Word, you find God's plan for your life, based on what He has done for you by sending Jesus as your Savior. As you read and study God's promises, they come alive more and more each day.

As you remember your Baptism, you see how God, in His love, called you as His very own. He adopted you into His family, gave you His name, and marked you with the cross of His Son. As you remember your Baptism, God calls you to repent of your sins, and He raises you above your old nature, which constantly works to separate you from God and His gift of new life. As your new self, which God created in you, daily emerges, the Holy Spirit works in you to nurture and develop your relationship with your heavenly Father.

In the gift of the Lord's Supper, your new life is nourished with the very body and blood of the one who made that new life possible—Jesus Christ. He gave Himself on the cross. Now He gives Himself in Holy Communion so your new life might grow and mature. Fed with this heavenly meal, you can serve Him joyfully in all areas of your life.

God has so much in store for you. It's hard to imagine all that you can do with your life if you explore the adventure *with* God rather than without Him. Just remember that you won't reach perfection here on earth. While you're down here, you're just "becoming." And remember, *becoming* means *growing*.

Becoming Involves Setting Goals

What targets are you aiming for in life? If you don't aim carefully, you may never hit the target. But it's far worse not to have a target. What do you want to be? What do you hope to accomplish? Unless you make some decisions, you may waste the best years of your life only to discover it's much more difficult to pursue other options.

Ask yourself where you want to go. Make a plan. Get a map. Talk to others about your plans and the options before you. Don't forget to take your questions and concerns to God. He has promised to guide you in everything you do. Don't spend your whole life going around in circles.

Compare your goals to the following list from a group of high school freshmen.

- **Go to college.** That's a great goal, but it only goes so far. As soon as you start college, you'll need to reevaluate your goal and set a new one. College really isn't a goal because it's not the end. It's just another step in the process of reaching a goal.

- **Make money.** It's pretty hard to live without money. Life is certainly more comfortable if you have enough cash to get what you want without worrying about the bills. But money isn't what matters most. It's what you *do* with money. Some of the unhappiest people have all the money they could ever want. Jesus often warned His followers—and us—about how easily money can get between a person and God. That's not to say that God wants you to be poor. Many faithful Christians have been rewarded with great wealth, but they had the right perspective. They didn't make money itself their goal. Money is a *tool* God gives you to help you achieve His plan for your life. Money is not a goal.

- **Have a fun job.** Now there's a tricky goal! Basically, it sounds like a good answer. Even though some people want to play around all their lives, most of us want to work, and we want our work to be interesting and worthwhile. How tragic that some people spend year after year doing things they hate or that bore them! Why do they put up with it? "Because I make good money," might be one answer. But wouldn't that be like selling yourself into slavery—you'll do anything as long as it pays enough? Why settle for that when there's so much you can do with your life?

- **Get into computer programming.** Now why would someone choose such a goal? "Because that's what my dad does, and he says there's always some new challenge," explained the student who offered this goal. What a great reason to set such a clear course for your life. Something good is happening when you have such high regard for your parents that you want to be like them. And it's good to have ambitions to keep learning and growing, tapping into the potential that God has given you.

- **Help others.** Young Christians care about others. It's wonderful that many Christian young people want to work toward a career that will help others. To become a nurse, doctor, dentist, social worker, psychologist, teacher, minister, or missionary is a truly worthy goal.

- **Tell others about Christ.** Happily some individuals set good goals that go beyond choosing a career. When you are filled with joy because of your new life in Christ, it's natural to want to share it. Because you really care about others, you want them to have what God has given to you. It doesn't matter what school you attend, where you live, how much or how little you have, or what your future vocation will be. You can be a dishwasher and share Christ. You can be an athlete and share Christ. The Good News is as powerful in the student commons as it is in the pulpit. A good friend can be as effective as a pastor when it comes to telling the Gospel message—maybe even more effective.

So what are your goals? Don't just copy those listed here or the goals your friends have set. You need to choose your own goals. They have to come out of your heart and mind. Don't be afraid that your goals won't be as good as someone else's. Every goal listed has potential. Whether the goal is good or bad is up to the person who sets the goal. Whether you ask God to be a part of achieving the goal makes the goal good. No accomplishment, no goal, will ever be "good" unless God has helped you achieve it. Remember, *becoming* requires that you set some goals.

Becoming Involves High Standards

Did you hear the one about the man who was fishing for trout in a mountain stream? He seemed to be catching more than the other fishermen. He already had several small trout in his creel before they had landed their first. Then he had a really good strike. The other fishermen could tell by the action of the line that he had a big one. The man reeled in the biggest fish of the day. Then he took out a ruler, measured the fish, and—much to the surprise and dismay of the other fishermen—threw it back into the water.

The next couple of fish the man caught were smaller. He kept them. Then he reeled in another large trout, which he measured and threw back. Well, the other fishermen were exasperated. One person finally got up the nerve to ask why he was being so foolish. "I only have a 10" frying pan. The two I threw back were too big for the pan," the man answered.

True or not, the story makes a point. Too many people, even a lot of young people, set their standards too low. And low standards generally mean no standards. If your standards are low enough, then nobody fails. But if your standards are that low, everybody loses.

Setting low standards, while not a recent development, has grown into a nationwide problem. Popular standards, especially those that govern the entertainment industry, seem to have sunk to new depths. Entertainment once meant going to the movies several times a month. You carefully selected the film, and a commonly accepted code assured that almost all movies met a decent moral standard. Today, many films center around shocking violence and portray immoral acts as acceptable.

In addition to movies, we now spend vast amounts of time enjoying television and radio. These media inject massive doses of low standards into every home. You can spend several hours every day watching one program after another. While many programs are good, well-written shows that provide a delightful way to relax or learn, you have to watch and listen carefully. Even though you could argue that TV is a great gift from God, when viewing programs from the perspective of your new life in Christ, you quickly recognize many problems. First cable and now even the major networks seem willing to go to any extreme to exploit sex and violence.

Many popular programs suggest that anything goes. Comedians joke about hangovers, drug trips, and sexually transmitted diseases, implying that alcohol, drugs, and promiscuous sex are not serious issues or destructive. Talk show hosts, motivated by their need to keep ratings high, constantly offer sensational, mind-numbing material. They expose the public to the off-beat and the controversial. Christians who believe, on the basis of God's Word, that homosexual relationships are wrong are ridiculed by gays who insist that their lifestyle must be given social approval. What can be even more damaging is the appearance of some radical minister or psychologist who speaks against traditional Christian positions. You rarely see a happily married couple or a stable family or a Christian individual presented in a positive light.

Situation comedies, movies, and plays often give a distorted, confusing picture of morality. Boy meets girl. Boy and girl like each other. By the end of the day, boy and girl are in bed together. Or husband and wife argue. Husband and wife do little to work through their problems. Husband and wife go their separate ways and find new lovers.

What's wrong with these story lines? Defenders of such questionable material argue that these are only stories. They aren't meant to teach anything. They're just for entertainment. But you know the danger. If you hear a lie often enough, you end up believing it—especially if you like the person telling the lie. Even ugly sins can look attractive if they're glamorized enough. Your defenses become weak as you are led to believe that "everybody's doing it." It becomes easy to overlook the fact that because others are doing it does not mean it's right.

And TV isn't the only offending medium. Inexpensive portable radios and CD players make it easy for you to carry your music with you wherever you go. Have you taken the time to really listen to the songs? Have you really evaluated the lyrics based on your new life in Christ?

Take a few minutes to evaluate the influence television and music have on your life. Would you feel comfortable inviting Jesus to watch your favorite movie or television program? Would you take Him along to hear your favorite music group?

Now that you've identified some potential bad influences on your new life in Christ, what can you do about it? Well, when a doctor examines a person and discovers a deadly, infectious disease, the doctor doesn't sit back and say, "Well, that's the way it is." She sends her patient for treatment. When doctors and nurses treat the patient, they wear sterile caps, gowns, and masks. They do what they can to get the patient healthy again, but they make every effort to avoid exposing themselves to the patient's disease.

That's how you need to approach your life. You have to set higher standards for yourself—you need to take every precaution to avoid exposing yourself to the temptations of the world. It's not easy. You have to ask God to help you take a stand against what's wrong, to fight what you know is sinful.

But who sets the standards? Who says what's right and wrong? How can you be certain that your standards are the right ones? If you took a poll, many people would say that the majority rules. In other words, if everybody's doing something, that makes it all right. It's like grading on a curve. If the average score is low, lower the curve, then there are always some *As*.

Who sets the standards? You already know the answer to that question—God sets the standards. No matter how you look at it, that's the only answer that makes sense. God planned, designed, and created our lives. As Creator, He did a fantastic job. Even the greatest geniuses in history haven't invented anything that comes close to what God has given us. As our Creator, God knows more about us than we do about ourselves.

Think of it this way. When you buy a new stereo, you get an instruction manual. Usually the envelope says something like "Important—Read before Using!" The manufacturer put a lot of thought, time, and expense into that stereo. Do you want good service and long life from it? Then pay attention to the instructions. The stereo can't be expected to do things it was never designed to do. If you don't follow the instructions, you're headed for trouble and probably an early break-down.

In your best interest, God has given you instructions to guide your life. They contain common sense standards and instructions for trouble-free years and a long and satisfying life. You know these standards well. In fact, you memorized the basics. You guessed it, they're the Ten Commandments. In the thousands of years since God gave them to Moses, no one has ever improved on them.

God designed the Big Ten of Exodus 20 to keep you from harm and danger. They're like the guardrails at the side of the road. A driver can willfully or carelessly ignore them, but twisted, rusting metal at the bottom of the hill is ample reminder that driving past them is not a smart idea.

Even though it's clear that God gave us the Ten Commandments to keep us from messing up and we can see that they would help us get the most out of life, many people still balk at them. They insist they have the right to live however they want. They head out in other directions. What happens when you ignore God's commands? Read on for a real-life example of the problems that can happen when you ignore the rules.

In 1980, a volcano in southern Washington threatened to erupt. A man named Harry Truman (not the former president!) had a small home and campground on this mountain next to a beautiful lake. When scientists issued their warning about the eruption, state and National Forest Service officials declared a large area around the mountain off-limits. Signs were posted. Campers, vacationers, hunters, and fishermen grumbled, but they obeyed the warnings. Nobody grumbled or complained more than Harry Truman. He refused to let anyone force him out of his home or off his land.

When the volcano finally blew its top, it destroyed a much larger area than expected. Even years later, miles of gray ash, a dirty gray river, and thousands of dead, toothpick-like trees litter the landscape. There was no trace of Mr. Truman or his former home and camp at Spirit Lake on Mt. St. Helens. His stubborn decision to ignore the warnings cost him his life.

When the off-limits signs were first posted at Mt. St. Helens, residents and visitors alike felt the government had gone too far. They were resentful that so much land had been roped off. They complained that the Forest Service and the state were being overcautious. But as it turned out, the complainers were wrong. The volcano's eruption caused the death of more than 60 people. Many of those killed had insisted on their right to get as close to the closed area as possible. Later, relatives and friends of the dead tried to sue the government, claiming that the authorities were negligent. They argued the state should have been tougher, it should have issued stronger warnings and imposed even tighter restrictions.

God has set life's standards. Many think the Ten Commandments are too narrow and restrictive. They brush them aside and do their own thing. But are they too narrow? Broken lives, broken homes, sick minds, diseased bodies, single parents, unwed mothers, alcoholics, and drug addicts can be found everywhere. This should be enough evidence to prove that God has been right all along—living His way is the only way to live.

Don't be surprised if you run into problems as you try to follow God's standards. God issued a warning about this a long time ago. It comes down to being different. There is a big difference between people who are alive in God and people who are not alive in God—between Christians and what Jesus calls "the world." That's why God included so many statements like these in the Bible:

> They [Jesus' disciples] are not of the world any more than I am of the world. *John 17:14*

They are from the world and therefore speak from the viewpoint of the world, and the world listens to them. We are from God, and whoever knows God listens to us; but whoever is not from God does not listen to us. This is how we recognize the Spirit of truth and the spirit of falsehood. *1 John 4:5–6*

Yes, there is a difference and sometimes even a conflict between believers and unbelievers. If you don't ask God to help you stand firmly in the faith, others may be able to impose their lower standards on you. You will begin making the same mistakes they make and paying the same penalties.

Do not conform! Remember that God has given you a new life and has made a complete change in you. Don't go back to lower standards. Move up to quality! Ask God to help you show in your daily life that you know His will and that you desire, more than anything else, to do His "good, pleasing and perfect will" (Romans 12:2). (While you're at it, why not read Romans 12 again? It gives you a lot to think about.) What's the best way to avoid being influenced by low standards? Stick with God's high standards. He will strengthen you to live by them.

Becoming Involves Commitment

The students in one high school selected "Committed to Excel" as their school motto. They chose to set their sights high. And they will reach even their highest goals if they are really committed to excellence.

"Committed to Excel"—that's a good goal for you too. But think it through first. Do you really know what *excel* means? It's not difficult to define. The dictionary says it means "to be superior to others in some good or desirable quality, attainment, or performance." *Excel* is essentially the same word as *excellent*. But it means more than just being superior to others, more than just "good" or "above average." *Excellent* is as close to *perfect* as we humans can get. *Excel* means trying to be the best that you can possibly be.

A second question: Do you really want to excel? Do you have a strong desire to be the best person, the best Christian, that you can possibly be? There is a big difference between daydreaming and planning. Daydreaming is wishful thinking. Planning involves making a decision and doing something about it. And there's a difference between a group decision and a personal decision. Personal decisions require you to be totally honest with yourself about your goals and what you will do to achieve them. Without total honesty, you could find yourself in an embarrassing situation.

For example, a young executive had an important business appointment with a prospective client. He wanted to come across as the best in the business, someone who knew all the important people. As the prospective client was ushered into his office, the executive was talking on the phone. He motioned to the man to be seated.

The prospective client couldn't help but overhear the executive's side of the conversation. "Yes, sir! We will be able to handle it without any trouble. It's a rather big order, but we are accustomed to doing things on a big scale. And don't worry about the state commission. I'll call the governor and straighten everything out."

As the executive hung up the phone, he smiled at the man and explained, "Sorry to keep you waiting, but it was a very important call." At just that moment, the secretary knocked on the door. She stuck her head in long enough to say, "I thought I should tell you, your phone is out of order. It should be fixed within an hour."

As you can see, dishonesty leads to embarrassment. And people who are phony about goals and standards never go anywhere. If you can't sell yourself on what you want to do and how you want to do it, you'll never work to achieve your goal. You will never excel.

A third question: Are you willing to pay the price of striving to excel? Being a Christian can cost a lot. It may mean saying no when everyone else is saying yes. It may mean having a different set of values than your friends. It may mean losing friends, perhaps even someone you think you love, because their standards don't fit in your life. Do you care enough about wanting to be what God wants you to be to make those sacrifices? Are you willing to take risks for God?

The fourth question is equally important: Are you willing to make a commitment to excel? Are you really determined, with God's help, to be the best person you can possibly be? Don't answer, "I think so." There is no "maybe" in commitment. You must make up your mind and stick with it. It's an every-day-of-the-week, every-hour-of-the-day effort.

But making the commitment to excel in your walk of faith isn't as difficult as it sounds. In your daily walk with God, you get to enjoy His company. And your enjoyment will increase the longer you spend time with Him. You will begin to see God's guidance and enjoy His love and power in ways you never dreamed possible. What's more, you will find that your life is filled with those wonderful gifts and blessings that are called the "fruit of the Spirit": love, joy, peace, patience, kindness, goodness, faithfulness, gentleness, and self-control (Galatians 5:22–23). For the Christian, walking with God becomes "doing what comes naturally."

As you strive to excel, you will quickly learn that your success isn't up to you. If it were, you would never achieve it. God helps you make that commitment to excel. Then He walks with you every step of the way, strengthening and encouraging you as you travel. Your parents, your church, and your true friends will be at your side too, giving you help and encouragement. And there's a secret you'll learn (maybe you've learned it already): "[You] can do everything through Him who gives [you] strength" (Philippians 4:13).

Are you committed to excel? Go for it! That's a part of your continued growth in Christ. It's what God wants for you as His special child.

6

When the Road Gets Rough

Don't you hate it when you're in-line skating on a well-paved path and you suddenly hit a stretch that's pitted with holes? What can you do about it? Do you refuse to go on?

Of course not! You probably slow down a little and watch carefully so you can jump the rocks and skate around the holes. You might get a few bumps and jolts, which you would rather have avoided, but you stick to the course because it takes you where you want to go. Eventually things will smooth out, and you will once again be rolling along.

Living your new life in Christ is like skating along that path. You learned in church and confirmation class that Christ means everything to you. You couldn't have heard better news. You discovered that Jesus has the answer to every question, that He is the solution to every problem. You felt yourself joyfully breezing down life's highway. You found out you are special in God's sight, that your Lord is with you all the way. Everything was joy, peace, and love. You were really riding high. Your walk with God was totally uplifting.

Then you discovered that your course through this wonderful new life wasn't elevated 10 feet above all the chuckholes and rocks and mud that had bothered you before. You were still running into the same problems. The bumps and jolts hurt just as much as they did before.

Now what? Do you pretend those rough spots aren't really there? Some people try to do that. They attempt not to gripe or cry. They ignore the reality. But make-believe has no place in real Christian living. Pretending there aren't problems doesn't solve anything. Asking God to help you honestly size up your problems and face them is the first step to overcoming them.

What should you do after you figure out what's wrong? Should you turn back? That's not the answer either. If you really set a goal and start out on the course to achieve it, and if you really *want* to achieve the goal, you can't quit. But many do. They back out the minute the road gets rough. If you can't stick with it through the rough spots, you're setting yourself up for failure.

Rather than let you quit, God constantly encourages you. He tells you, "Be strong!" "Be faithful to death!" "Persevere!" He promises you will make it. God will see to it that you do.

Christians have expressed this encouragement in catchy phrases like: "When the going gets tough, the tough get going." Or "Tough times never last, but tough people do." Even though you may run into problems along the path of life, Jesus walked the rough path for you. He made it safely to the goal. He won forgiveness and eternal life for you on the cross. He's the answer to rough spots.

> Even though I walk through the valley of the shadow of death, I will fear no evil, for You are with me. *Psalm 23:4*

Always keep this in mind: Even if the path gets rough, keep going—carefully, prayerfully, hopefully, trustingly. You aren't traveling alone. If you hit a spot that seems impassable or impossible, your all-wise God will show you a way. Your all-powerful God will help you through it. So travel on in faith.

Admit it. God has given you an excellent path to follow. The daily and eternal blessings you enjoy along the way reduce the power and significance of your problems to nothing. God has filled your life with a lot of sunshine. Don't get upset when the clouds and rain come along. The rain doesn't undo the good that the sun does. God uses both the sun and the rain as a winning combination to nourish and enrich life.

If it rains on your parade, don't sit and sulk and feel sorry for yourself. Don't console yourself by repeating, "Into each life some rain must fall." When the bad weather cramps your style, remember, "This too shall pass." Wait out the storm and look joyfully for the new growth that will take place in your tomorrow.

The problems that turn up along life's road come in all shapes and sizes. You'll have no trouble recognizing them when they occur. But there is something you will discover, or maybe you already have. The problem really isn't the major issue. What you do about the problem—how you handle it—is more important.

Dodge the Potholes of Acceptance

Probably the biggest problem you'll face is feeling accepted. Most young people run into this pothole. But don't think it's a problem unique to teenagers. Feeling accepted is a basic, positive human desire. It's the way God made us. We all want to be loved and appreciated, no matter how old or how young we are.

The older you get, the greater your need to be accepted seems to become. Clubs, groups, societies, fraternities, and sororities spring up. Each has its own character and purpose. Each attracts one particular type of person. Some people are willing to pay a high price to belong, to be accepted. You probably identify these people as members of "in" groups. And in your neighborhood, you may run into gangs, each with its own territory that it defends from "others."

The existence of an in-group indicates that others are shut out. Even Christian groups on a high school or college campus could be considered in-groups, but if these groups work to serve the Lord, they shouldn't be shutting others out. Instead, they should be attracting newcomers and drawing them into fellowship through love, support, and sharing the Gospel message.

While a Christian group should be a positive example of an in-group, most in-groups seem to be snobbish. Whether you are "in" depends on what kind of car you drive, the clothes you wear, or your hair or makeup style. And the demands always change. The groups bounce from leather jackets to

T-shirts, from miniskirts to designer jeans, from long hair to no hair. Frankly, there's nothing wrong with these "fashion statements." The problem comes if you set standards to form a clique that shuts others out or puts others down. The problem multiplies when the standards of the in-group are morally low. Most problems with sex, drugs, and alcohol develop because of the overwhelming desire for acceptance.

Christian young people know better than to fool around with these things, but there is always the temptation to give in to the pressure and join the in-group. No one wants to appear different, not even Christian teenagers who *are* different because of their new life. But do you see where the problem is? Sure, the movers and pushers create a lot of influence, but don't blame them for your willingness to conform. The problem is in you.

Have you ever had a bonfire on an ocean beach? If you have, you probably gathered dry driftwood. Some of that driftwood probably was in the ocean a long time. If you examine it closely, you may find that marine worms have burrowed into the wood and barnacles have attached themselves to it. These creatures were looking for security so they attached themselves and their whole future to what appeared to be a strong, solid home.

These animals never dreamed their home was just a piece of driftwood that would end up in a fire.

Are you going to attach yourself to today's fickle in-groups because others are doing it and you want to be accepted? Don't conform! Don't give in to peer pressure! Don't compromise your faith! As God's special person, it's far more important to stay "in" with Christ. It may feel as though you are walking alone, but believe me, you aren't. Your walk with Christ is really worth it. It's part of being His special person.

Vault Over the Barrier of Competition

You also might run into problems with competition. Again, competition itself isn't bad. Like the desire to be accepted, it can have a positive effect on people. After all, wouldn't a game be pretty boring if no one tried to win? That applies to any game or sport—chess, card games, baseball, tennis, basketball, swimming. Remember how disgusted you were when you first discovered that adults were letting you win, that you really weren't as good at the game as you thought? The game wasn't fun anymore.

Competition can be bad, however, if your only goal is to beat someone else, not to play a good game or get good grades. Once again you see that whether competition is good or bad is up to you. It's your attitude and action that matters most. You determine whether competition becomes a problem or a blessing.

You don't have to be able to do everything or be able to do things better than others. That has nothing to do with whether you succeed or fail in life. God has given you a wide assortment of gifts, but He hasn't given everyone the same gifts to the same degree. Some of your friends are extremely artistic and creative. Some have super IQs. Some people you know can sing like birds. Some have exceptional athletic ability. One of your friends may be an all-star on the football field but a real klutz on the tennis court. You can't keep up with everybody. Don't even try.

Don't think of winning as always beating others. Instead, compete against yourself. Golfers do that as they try to better their own best scores. Artists, composers, and writers do that as they strive to make their newest composition their best. Runners, skaters, and swimmers do that as they pace each other to force that extra record-breaking burst of speed. Students do that as they try to master a subject. When you compete against yourself, you build yourself up without tearing anyone else down. The right kind of competition isn't a threat; it's a challenge. It stimulates and motivates. Don't back away from such challenges. Use them to grow.

As you face challenges, don't expect too much of yourself—or others. While perfection is a worthy goal and the ultimate hope of every Christian, don't become disappointed or depressed because you can't attain it. Some day you will be perfect. That's part of the crown of glory Jesus has promised to give to all His faithful followers. Here on earth, you need to ask your heavenly Father to help you keep striving for your goals, whether physical, mental, or spiritual. Then keep trying to do the best you can. And whether you succeed or fall short, you can count on the forgiving love of Jesus to get you past your shortcomings.

Break Through the Roadblock of Self-Indulgence

As you walk through your new life, you will probably encounter the roadblock of self-indulgence. As a toddler, you insisted on getting everything you wanted. You didn't know any better. As you grew up, your parents insisted that you share, that you put the interests of others before your own. Now that you're entering an adult world, you might realize that "looking after your own best interests" or "taking care of Number 1" is really just a nice way of referring to self-indulgence. And this extreme self-interest seems to be going on everywhere you look.

Satan knows self-interest is the weakest point in the human armor. When he tempts you, he doesn't prod you to do something you consider glaringly offensive. He doesn't come with a direct frontal attack. He finds those little cracks in your character and goes to work on them. The devil looks for those areas where you will be able to reason and excuse and justify your actions.

Check out your own life. Be your own private eye. Maybe you don't like math so you didn't study enough for the exam. You know cheating is wrong, but if you don't cheat—just this once, of course—you'll get a low grade. And maybe that poor grade will lower your grade point average and you won't get into college. Or maybe that poor grade will mean makeup work and you'll miss that camping trip with your friends. So you cheat. You know what Satan says? "Gotcha!"

Or maybe your boyfriend or girlfriend comes on pretty strong: "If you really love me, you'll make love to me." You remember the warnings from your parents. You don't want to ignore them. But you're afraid of losing this person. Then you start to think about how your favorite television character would react. You remember your friends talking about how everybody is doing it. You have sex, but you end up with a guilty conscience and a lot of fear. Your relationship probably falls apart. You may begin to doubt yourself. You may feel all alone with nowhere to turn. You're sorry for your decision. Remember, God is with you. He will forgive you—even for having premarital sex—because of Jesus' redeeming work.

Remember, there are two sets of standards in the world. One set is God's; the other is the world's. Ask God to help you stick to your commitment to follow His standards. You can't play it both ways. You can't play on two opposing teams at the same time. You end up losing both ways.

The world will pamper your big "I." It keeps exploring and exploiting drugs, alcohol, sex, love, and friendship—always searching for new highs because the old ones have become boring. But self-indulgence only leaves you disillusioned, wondering how you could get so far away from God—wondering if God could possibly take you back. But He will. Just ask God for forgiveness. Because of Jesus, you can be assured that you have it.

Leap the Hurdle of Fear

No doubt as you walk through life, you'll need to hurdle your fear of failure. Many young people are held back by it. Many never try anything new or big because they're afraid they won't make it. There's an old saying that says, "It is better to have loved and lost than never to have loved at all." You can say much the same about trying: "It is better to have tried and failed than never to have tried at all."

Believe it or not, you've already tried and failed many times in your life, but that didn't hold you back. Although you were too young to realize it, you failed often as you learned to walk. You got up and wobbled and fell. Despite failing, you didn't quit. You got up and fell, got up and fell. But you kept at it until one day you were strong enough and sure enough to stand and walk without falling.

You even failed as you were learning to talk. As you tried to communicate by imitating the words and sounds you heard, your family and friends laughed, even though they loved every sound you made and urged you to keep trying. Eventually you learned a few simple words, baby talk, that only your family could understand. Gradually you learned the meanings of new words and spoke in sentences. Now you know the rules of English and can clearly communicate your needs and dreams. But all this has come through trial and error.

Persistence pays off. Did you know that Abraham Lincoln lost seven elections? If he had backed down after the first one or even the sixth, he never would have become one of our greatest presidents. And Walt Disney's first business wasn't an immediate success. There were times when he was flat broke and couldn't even afford a decent place to live. But he had dreams and goals, and he never let his failures hold him back.

Don't be afraid to try new, more difficult things. It's not a disgrace to be a beginner. Everyone is a beginner at one time. Plan your goals. Set your sights on your goals. Then move out, asking God for His guidance and help.

Setting goals and moving forward confidently also applies to your Christian faith and life. It's not easy to be a Christian, not now or at any other time in your life. But don't give up. Don't say, "What's the use? I'll never make it anyway." Some people sit in their self-made ruts and complain, saying, "I never get any breaks. Even God doesn't give me a break." What a pity. It isn't "breaks" that they need. It's a clearer vision and a stronger faith. They've dug themselves in with their own fears and doubts.

Don't be afraid of tomorrow. Don't be afraid of the new and the uncertain. Don't belittle yourself. And don't belittle God who made you a special person. Ask Him to strengthen your faith so that you can once again go forward boldly and confidently. Believe with Paul: "I can do everything through Him who gives me strength" (Philippians 4:13).

But what if you do fail? Well, you won't be the first. It's not that failure doesn't matter or isn't serious. It does matter, and it is serious. But God has the answer and the cure. Only He has it, and only He gives it. You won't find it anywhere else.

The answer, the cure, is Jesus Christ. He turns your failures into victories. Because of God's gift of faith, Jesus' perfect life becomes your perfect life in God's sight. Your failures no longer exist because Jesus died and rose again to erase those failures.

Your attitude generally affects how you view problems. If you attempt to solve your problems on your own, you won't succeed. But if your attitude towards problems is to turn to God for the answers and solutions, you'll succeed. Why? Because God responds with an attitude of love. That's truly remarkable! God loves you despite your sins and failures. He has every reason to be disappointed with you, but He still loves you.

Best of all, God put His attitude of love into

action for you. He knows you even better than you know yourself. He knows your struggle with sin and temptation. He knows you'll never be perfect on your own. He knows the penalty you would have had to pay if the burden and guilt of your sin hadn't been removed. So God acted. He sent His Son, Jesus, to be your Savior. Jesus fulfilled God's perfect plan of salvation. By faith in Jesus, you are a full member of God's family. You are fully capable of success because God is at work in you.

What's the greatest joy you have as a special person in God's sight? It's that Christ took your burden and guilt of sin on Himself and paid the price. It cost Jesus His life to redeem you, but His great love for you made Him willing to pay that price. The threat of judgment no longer hangs over you. Your account is settled. It is marked, "Paid in full."

Someone may point the finger at you after you fail and say, "God will get you for that!" But you can turn around and say, "He could, but He won't. He's already forgiven me for Jesus' sake." That's not a glib way of passing over your failures. It's one way of confessing that Jesus is your Lord and Savior and showing that you know you're forgiven. And the next time you're tempted, with God's help, you will try not to make the same mistake.

Life's Greatest Treasure

Throughout life, we look for the greatest treasure, the greatest joy, the greatest victory, the greatest goal. What you have discovered in your new life with Christ is that you have all those things already. You have Jesus!

A man once met a traveler from a far country. The foreigner was wearing the most beautiful jewel the man had ever seen. He decided then and there that he would have such a jewel too. So the man traveled to far places, beginning with the homeland of the stranger. He trekked across barren deserts and slashed his way through dense jungles. He dredged icy streams and tunneled into craggy mountains, always searching for that jewel.

Finally, he came home empty-handed. He felt sad and defeated. The man had spent his life savings on the search. As he sat in silence in his own yard, lamenting his wasted life, he noticed a glint of light reflecting off a stone buried in the ground. He picked up the stone and discovered it was the same kind of precious gem he had been searching for—and it was right in his own yard. And there were others too. They had been there all the time, but because they were rough and weathered on the outside, he had never seen them for what they were.

Don't make that mistake with your new life in Christ. The grass is not greener on the other side of the fence. You have God on your side. You have Christ on your side. You are part of God's family of faith. And God promises to keep you with Him forever.

7

You Don't Have to Go It Alone

Although the road may be rough and the going may seem hard, you have set your course. As you ask God to help you follow His clear direction, you can be assured you are going the right way. As you trust in God's sure promise, you know you will get through all right. But there's another reason for you to keep going with confidence: You don't have to go it alone.

Feeling alone is one of the saddest situations anyone has to endure. Even at the beginning God never planned for anyone to be alone. "It is not good," He said and immediately provided for companionship, marriage, and family. Everyone has a need for private time and private space, but we all need other people. Above all, we need God.

Your yearning for companionship or friendship will continue throughout your life. As a tiny child, frightened at the howling wind, the flashing lightning, and the booming thunder, you lay in bed, hoping someone would come sit with you. As soon as your mother or father sat on your bed, you relaxed and fell peacefully asleep. Or consider an older person confined to his house. He sits in the same room day after day, month after month. Life becomes monotonous; even television is boring. One thing brings a spark and sparkle back to his life—the visit of a relative or friend.

A song from several years ago stated that "People who need people are the luckiest people in the world." It's true. It isn't easy to go it alone. In fact, no one wants to be alone. This also applies to your Christian faith and living your life God's way. It can be difficult to follow Christ if you feel you are the only one who cares, the only one who's really trying.

One of God's prophets once felt so alone that he told God he didn't want to live anymore. He was trying so hard to share God's message with others, but nothing ever happened. At least that's how it seemed to him. He felt he was wasting his life—trying to do the impossible—and it wasn't worth it. Everybody was against him.

What Elijah didn't know was that he wasn't alone. He wasn't wasting his time. God *was* with him. God told Elijah that there were 7,000 other believers right in his own neighborhood. Seven thousand people who were on the same side, who felt and believed as Elijah did. These people were faithful to God, just as he was. Read about Elijah again, especially the exciting events in 1 Kings 18 and 19.

You aren't alone either, even though you may feel that way at times. You don't walk the Christian path alone. God walks with you. But when tough times and rough roads come, where do you find your help? To whom can you turn?

A group of Christian high school students was asked that question. It wasn't surprising that the immediate and almost unanimous answer was "my friends." Like everyone else, you need one or two special people that you feel close to. You like the same things. You like each other. You enjoy doing things together. You trust each other. You feel you can share your dreams and secrets with each other. You feel you really understand each other.

Naturally, when the road gets rough, you look to your friends for help. You feel you can depend on them, otherwise they probably wouldn't be your friends. If you don't get the help you need, you might feel your friends have disappointed you. You might feel betrayed. You might feel that those people weren't really true friends.

Thank God for your friends! But don't expect your friends to have all the answers. They usually are in the same boat as you. More than likely, they haven't experienced or learned any more than you have. Sometimes the very worst advice you can get will come from your friends. They mean well, but they just don't know what's best for you. That's especially true when they don't believe in Jesus or understand that God has a plan for your life.

Don't sell your friends short, however. You need them. The very fact that you have so much in common is helpful. But for your own good, don't think of friends as the only source of help.

The same group of students was asked who else they would turn to for help. After a few moments of thought-filled silence, several answered that they would go to their brothers or sisters. That's a good answer too—especially when you have an older brother or sister. They probably experienced the same things several years ago. Older brothers and sisters can tell you how they handled the situation or the problem and how to avoid any mistakes they might have made.

Perhaps the best reason to seek the advice of your brothers and sisters is that they have known and loved you all your life. They understand you a lot better than you think. Friends can walk away from you and forget about your needs, but your brother or sister lives with you every day. Your life affects theirs. Your decisions affect theirs. It's almost as important to them that you get things worked out right as it is to you.

But are those the only people the students turned to for help? Several students answered that they went to their parents. That response caused a low murmur in the room. From the comments that were made, it was obvious that everyone agreed they *should* turn to their parents for help and advice. It was also obvious that some of them didn't. Why not?

A couple students said their parents never took their problems seriously. They belittled them and brushed them off. The students felt their parents were too busy to listen. When they did listen, it seemed as though their parents were just trying to get it over with in a hurry. "They just don't understand!" was an often-repeated phrase.

Other students said their parents took their problems too seriously. They made too big a deal out of everything, making mountains out of mole-hills. Even after the problem was over, these students' parents still talked and worried about it. Again the kids said, "They just don't understand!"

Of course, some students admitted that they considered their parents to be friends. They could go to their parents with anything and find the counsel, help, and encouragement they needed. This response brought calls of "You're lucky!" from others in the room.

Let's face it, your parents care more about you than anyone else in the world. They've made many sacrifices for you throughout your life so you can have what you need. They will continue to make sacrifices for the rest of their lives. If you feel you can't talk things over with your parents, you are missing something special. Sit down with them. Share with them what other young people have said and felt. See if you can't get your act together as a family. You really need each other.

To be perfectly honest, if there is a communication gap between you and your parents, it may be more your fault than theirs. You cannot expect your parents to understand you if you aren't totally up front with them. Give your parents a chance.

You'd be amazed at how much they know, how much they love you, and how much help they can provide.

The same advice holds true of your pastor. Interestingly, not one of the students in that fairly large group of Christians said they had ever gone to their pastor with a personal problem. Don't overlook that source of help. You'll find that your pastor has a tremendous love and a deep understanding for the people he serves—even the young people.

Because he deals with human problems all the time, your pastor is in a great position to help you over and around life's rough spots. And he doesn't lead a sheltered life; he knows what's going on. Your pastor also knows God and His forgiving love. He can be a huge help in strengthening you in your walk with God. For your own sake, get to know your pastor better. He can be a great friend.

While these students listed people from whom they would seek help, they also listed the best source of help—God. Your loving Lord should mean the most to you and should be the first place you turn for the answers to every one of life's problems and rough spots.

You can trust God when He says that you don't have to go it alone. He has told you "Be strong and courageous. Do not be terrified; do not be discouraged, for the LORD your God will be with you wherever you go" (Joshua 1:9). And Jesus told you, "Surely I am with you always" (Matthew 28:20). If you feel like you're all alone, remember this phrase: "If you feel far from God, guess who moved?" Ask God to assure you of His never-ending presence in your life. He will walk with you the entire way.

Ask God to send His Spirit to keep you close to Him. You can't do it on your own. When the Holy Spirit opens your heart, you will learn that God is constantly giving you signals and assurances of His presence through His Word. And your church helps keep you informed of God's guidance by keeping you in touch with God's Word and the Sacraments. If your family holds daily devotions, that's another excellent way to keep tuned in to God. Obviously, your private Scripture reading and prayer time is yet another way God works in your life to keep you close to Him.

All these practices nourish your faith the same way nutritious meals strengthen your body. It's almost impossible to stay healthy without a steady diet of quality food. It is equally impossible to stay spiritually healthy without a daily intake of the spiritual food God offers in His Word and Sacraments. An occasional nibbling, a once-a-week church service, is not enough.

Do you know someone who is anorexic? People with this illness can literally waste away. Their bones may almost protrude through their skin, making them look like living skeletons. This disease isn't caused by a germ or virus. In most cases, it stems from very low self-esteem. First, they decide they are too fat. Then they decide not to eat. And then the anorexia takes over and they can no longer eat. Without help, anorexics will die. The help these people need goes beyond intravenous feeding. They need an entire attitude adjustment. They have to redevelop a will to live and a greater sense of self-esteem.

Many young people lose their sense of being God's special children. In an effort to be like everyone else, they downplay their new life in Christ and start skipping opportunities to feed on His Word or eat at His Table. It doesn't take long before they lose their appetite for God's Word and His friendship. This rejection of God is a matter of personal attitude, not peer pressure or personal problems. If something doesn't happen to restore the person's appetite for a relationship with the Lord, faith could be lost forever.

This can't be emphasized enough: The things that happen around you do not determine how strong your faith is. What matters is how deeply you are "rooted and established" in Christ (Ephesians 3:17).

Think of it this way. There is a beautiful rain forest on the Olympic Peninsula in western Washington. The area experiences high rainfall, and the ocean stabilizes the temperature. Every factor is favorable for healthy, steady growth, but the ground is littered with fallen logs. Why? There is so much water on the surface that the trees don't have to send down deep roots. In fact, the roots lie almost on top of the ground. When strong winds blow, these surface roots can't hold the trees. Despite their health and apparent strength, the trees fall. They can't stand against the pressure of the wind because they don't have deep roots.

On the other hand, high in the Sierra Nevada mountains of central California, there's another forest—of bristlecone pines. Botanists believe that they are probably the oldest living things in North America. For centuries these scrubby trees have fought to stay alive. Where they grow, the soil is sparse and rocky. Rainfall is meager. To stay alive, the pines send roots deep into the crevices and fissures of the rocks—some to remarkable depths. At times the winds blow mercilessly across the mountains, but these little trees are anchored so deeply into the rock that even the fiercest blasts seem not to harm them. The bristlecone pine may not look stately or impressive, but it has lived a long life.

Your whole future—even your eternal future—depends on how deeply rooted you are in the love of Christ. Sometimes as you look at the clouds on the horizon and size up your strength, you feel helpless and alone. But you aren't alone. Jesus is right there with you. It's like the "Footprints" story says, when the going gets rough, Jesus picks you up and carries you through.

Jesus assured His disciples that nothing could stand in the way of God's perfect plan. His words gave them—and us—hope and vision:

> With man this is impossible, but not with God; all things are possible with God. *Mark 10:27*

That's the beauty of being a Christian. You don't have to go it alone. In fact, you can't go it alone. Jesus has done it all for you and promises to be with you every step of the way.

8

No One Should Have to Go It Alone

As special as you are, you aren't the only one God loves. You aren't the only one for whom Jesus came and died. There are many people out there. Your friends have their hurts and problems too. They hate being alone. They also need and want the hope and life that only God can give. It takes someone who knows and has God's love to share that love with them—someone like you!

> This is how we know we are in Him: Whoever claims to live in Him must walk as Jesus did.
> *1 John 2:5–6*

While it's important to get a steady stream of nutritious spiritual food so that your faith can grow strong, you also need to think about what you do *after* God has given you this food and strengthened you. You have a couple choices. You can sit around, do very little, and let that healthy food turn into fat, or you can work and exercise and become even stronger. Consider these three examples of people who didn't avoid tough situations but faced them with God's help and came through with a stronger faith.

Many years ago, a nun was moved to tears by the sight of starved, emaciated people dying on the streets of Calcutta, India. She and several other nuns found a place where they could take those near death and give them loving attention during their last days. Over the years, the work of this woman and her organization grew until the world finally took notice. Her unselfish devotion and service to the poor and the outcasts of society have made her one of the truly great people of our day.

In 1979, the activities of Mother Teresa earned her a Nobel Peace Prize. This humble, frail woman was honored for her big heart and big faith. Although she was probably happy that the world had recognized the importance of her work, she was personally embarrassed about all the fuss.

Hawaiians have a similar high regard for Father Damien, a Belgian priest who ministered to lepers on the island of Molokai during the 1800s. The priest was a young, healthy man when he chose to live with and serve the residents of the Kalaupapa Leper Settlement. It must have been difficult to work constantly with people whose flesh gradually became numb and dead and whose fingers, toes, and noses would eventually rot away! But Father Damien had one conviction: These people needed to know about God's love. They needed to find hope in Him. Father Damien felt God had called him to this ministry.

One day as Father Damien enjoyed a cup of coffee, he spilled some on his foot. As he mopped up the spill, he realized that he hadn't felt any pain. He gathered those in the settlement that he ministered to and said, "Now I am one of you!" It never occurred to Father Damien that the disease might hamper his ministry. He didn't feel sorry for himself. What mattered most was that he could now identify even more fully with his "flock" and perhaps be better able to serve them.

Years ago, a young man was sent to prison. He had lived selfishly and broken many laws while "looking after his own best interests." Imprisonment was harder than he had expected. A prison chaplain visited the young man. The chaplain talked with the young man about God and His love for sinners. By God's grace, the young man believed that Jesus is his Savior. God's gift of faith completely changed the young man's life.

After his release from prison, this young man adopted a very open attitude about his faith. He lives a life consistent with his new life in Christ. This man also is concerned about those who still live on the wrong side of the law. He counsels those in trouble. He regularly writes to former prisoners, witnessing to them of the wonderful life God has for them. The Holy Spirit has worked through this man's witness to bring many people to faith in Jesus.

These may be above-average examples of what can happen when you ask Christ to help you live your new life to the fullest, but these three people exhibit the truth of what God has promised. He will bless your activities and work through your message of the Good News to bless others.

While you may think these are isolated stories or that these events are a bit removed from your life, think about this. God has given each of us our own arena, our own area of activity. And we are never alone in it. Others constantly interact with us. Their needs are the opportunities that God provides for us to serve. You have the chance to serve God and others by using your unique talents.

How do you do this? Well, first you need to move past the help-the-little-old-lady-across-the-street good deeds. Certainly you can welcome the chance to visit those confined to nursing homes, to do the shopping or mow the lawn for a sick neighbor, or to baby-sit for the busy mom who needs a night out. These are all good things to do. Such gestures of goodwill can be true expressions of Christian love. But they should be done freely, willingly, and joyfully as an important part of your new life in Christ. These deeds are prompted by Christ's example and by a genuine response to the love God has shown you.

Your Role in Your Family

Loving as Christ loved—that's the basic formula. Follow that formula in your family life. Everyone in your family owes love and respect to everyone else. But the roles that love demands of each family member may differ. Your parents' roles, as set by God, are ones of guide, trainer, and disciplinarian. Thank God if they consistently fulfill their duties.

Think about this example. A high school senior brought her friend to see her pastor. "Pastor, will you help her?" she asked. "She's really messed up!" And the girl *was* messed up. Her grades were horrible. She was experimenting with smoking, drinking, and drugs. The tough crowd at school considered her an easy mark, and the straight kids didn't like her. Actually, she didn't like herself either.

As the pastor spoke with her, the young woman poured out her heart. "I wish my mother loved me. Susan's mother loves her. She's strict. When Susan goes out, her mother wants to know where she's going, who she'll be with, and what she'll be doing. Then Susan's mother tells her when she expects her to be home. Her mother really cares about her!

"But my mother doesn't care about me at all. She lets me do whatever I want. So I end up doing bad things—things I really don't want to do—just to force her to say something. But she never does!"

Thank God if you have parents who care, who live up to the responsibilities that God requires of parents. Love them. Honor them. Work with them, not against them. Your parents may not always be right. If you feel they are wrong, level with them. Talk things through, but don't ignore them or disobey them. Obedience is the highest proof of love and respect that you can give your parents. And it's what God expects from you. Ask Him to help you fulfill your responsibilities to them.

You probably remember this from confirmation class, but in case you don't, the Fourth Commandment is the only commandment that carries a promise from God. If you choose to ignore God's command to honor your parents—whether at home, school, or wherever else—you will be in constant conflict. If you ask God to help you obey this command, you will taste the joys of peace and harmony.

Just remember, your family is a team. Every person on the team must be concerned about the good of the whole team. This kind of team spirit wins. If you don't believe me, look at your favorite professional sport. Each year a couple athletes think that they are real superstars. They seem to focus on increasing their own performance records and getting as many personal endorsements as possible. They expect management and even teammates to cater to them and play around them. They act as though they are too good to make sacrifices for others.

Inevitably, these non-team superstars burn out. When they refuse to follow the coach's directions, they get benched. Eventually management will trade them away. It's better not to have these players than to pay the price for their ego trips.

Unfortunately, a family doesn't have the option of removing members who think the world revolves around them. The family is stuck with the situation. But why does that have to be the situation? Young people who demand the right to do whatever they want show the worst kind of immaturity and self-indulgence. Adults who let them get away with it show the worst kind of parental responsibility. Nobody wins; everybody loses.

That's the heartache God was trying to spare you and your family when He moved St. Paul to write:

> Children, obey your parents in the Lord, for this is right. "Honor your father and mother"— which is the first commandment with a promise—"that it may go well with you and that you may enjoy long life on the earth."
> *Ephesians 6:1–3*

Your Role as a Friend

You also need to be a responsible Christian within your circle of friends. Just as it is important that you have good friends, it is also important that you *be* a good friend. You know the power your friends have on you. You also know that this influence can be good or bad. You have seen many "good" people get into trouble because they stuck with the wrong kind of friends. You have also seen how "successful" people can be with the right kind of friends.

True friendship is very important. Where do you find it? Actually it starts with you. If you are honest and consistent in your walk with Christ, you will attract people to you. Of course, others may avoid you because you're a Christian. Don't let rejection bother you. Remember, many turned away from Jesus too. Being consistent in your Christian faith and life will attract the right kind of friends. You can depend on one another, and that is important.

As a friend, you need to be a true beacon for your companions, and they need to be one for you. You need to know that you can count on one another. If the signals you give aren't consistent, your friends will be confused. They could get hurt because they put their trust in you. They may feel you have betrayed them. The following story demonstrates this point.

> A Coastguard pilot steered a small patrol boat up the St. Lawrence River late on a foggy night. He proceeded slowly and cautiously because of the low visibility. His charts showed the locations of all the navigational lights. He followed them carefully mile after mile. At one point he became a bit confused. He saw the next light

clearly, but it didn't match his calculations of boat and river current speed. He decided to trust the light and changed his course according-ly. A sudden jolt followed by a crunch shook the boat. It had run aground.

What happened? An investigation showed that the light the pilot thought was the navigation-al aid was actually the light of a moving freight train on a track parallel to the river. It was an honest mistake, but the pilot paid for it.

But it isn't just your friends who get hurt if you send confusing signals. You can get hurt too. People who mean the most to you may no longer trust you the way they did. They may no longer feel close to you.

Your inconsistency will also affect those who avoid you because of your Christian faith. Whether these people like you, they probably respect you as someone who remains true to his or her convic-tions. Down deep, some of these "enemies" may hope you are right. They long for your positive faith. They see something good in you. If you send mixed signals, they may jump to the conclusion that what Christ offers can't be that great. If it was, you would never turn your back on it.

Young Christians need true friends. They also need opportunities for positive, wholesome activi-ties. Being a Christian does not mean sacrificing fun and games. You can have as much fun as anybody, but you should choose your activities just as you choose your friends—wisely. You can have lively parties, but they shouldn't be marred by drugs or alcohol or sex. Be a leader for your friends in the activities you choose.

Your church can be a big help when it comes to choosing acceptable activities. Some teenagers complain about their church youth activities. But give them a chance. Don't just go and sit like a bump on a log, waiting for someone else to do all the planning and provide the entertainment. If you do that, you have no right to criticize. If you want something good, then get involved and make something good happen. Your pastor and youth counselors will work with you. But you have to talk with them; they aren't mind readers. They can help you find what you need and want only if you open up to them and work with them to develop a good youth program.

One of the great joys of being God's special person is knowing that you aren't alone. God is with you and so are thousands, even millions, of God's people. While you need them, don't forget they need you too.

9

Tomorrow Is Today

There are a lot of tomorrows in your life. College may be a tomorrow for you. A career, a profession, or a job may be a tomorrow. Going steady may be a tomorrow. Even a first date may be a tomorrow. Very likely marriage is. Sometimes as you replay these hopes and dreams, you impatiently ask, "Why can't it happen today? Why do I always have to wait?"

That's one good thing about being a Christian. You don't have to deal with a lot of "tomorrows" or "some days." It doesn't make any difference how old you are or where you are in life, as a Christian, *tomorrow is today*. Thanks to Jesus, you have everything—faith, hope, life, the Spirit, everything you could ever need or want—today.

Because of Jesus, you don't have to spend even a day wondering how to get right with God. You don't have to pray, "Create in me a pure heart, O God," and then wait for it to happen *some day.* Thanks to Jesus, it's already happened. The peace of forgiveness is already yours—today.

Because of Jesus, you don't have to spend even a day worrying that death will end everything. Christ has already conquered death and given you this promise, "Be faithful, even to the point of death, and I will give you the crown of life" (Revelation 2:10). Eternal life is yours—a promise you can cling to now and that will be fulfilled when you die.

It all comes back to this business of being special. You are truly special in God's sight. Christ has made you special. You are God's child. Notice that wasn't "You *will be* God's child." You are God's child *right now.*

One Christmas Eve a Sunday school superintendent received a telephone call from the mother of the boy who was going to play Joseph in the children's service. The child was sick and wouldn't be able to participate. The superintendent and several teachers quickly put their heads together. Who could they get to replace Joseph? They finally decided the simplest solution was to write Joseph out of the script. There was no Joseph that night. Nobody even noticed.

Maybe there are times when you feel like that. God could write you out of the script and nobody would ever know the difference. You just don't feel very important. But this isn't true. God had a significant role for Joseph in the Christmas story. It may not seem as essential as that of Jesus or Mary, but if you read Matthew 1, you will see how important Joseph was.

God has a significant role for you too. It will be interesting and exciting to watch it unfold. Don't sell yourself short because you won't be another apostle like Peter or Paul. God brought them into the world exactly when He needed them. Don't sit back because you don't see yourself as a reformer like Martin Luther or a missionary like David Livingstone. God put them in the world just when He needed them.

You are right here, right now, because God needs you here. He has chosen you and put you just where He wants you. He has made you a special person, and He has an important role for you to fulfill. You aren't an understudy, waiting to step into someone else's shoes. God has written this role—your role—specifically for you. No one will write you out of the script. You aren't waiting in the wings. You are already center stage—right now—today!

The curtain has gone up! **You're on!**